POSITION AND DIRECTION

Claire Piddock

Crabtree Publishing Company

www.crabtreebooks.com

Author: Claire Piddock
Publishing plan research and development:
  Sean Charlebois, Reagan Miller
  Crabtree Publishing Company
Editor: Molly Aloian
Editorial director: Kathy Middleton
Project coordinator: Margaret Salter
Prepress technician: Margaret Salter
Coordinating editor: Chester Fisher
Series editor: Jessica Cohn
Project manager: Kumar Kunal (Q2AMEDIA)
Art direction: Rahul Dhiman (Q2AMEDIA)
Cover design: Shruti Aggarwal (Q2AMEDIA)
Design: Sajid Mohmmad, Cheena Yadav (Q2AMEDIA)
Photo research: Ekta Sharma (Q2AMEDIA)

Photographs:

Shutterstock: Jacek Chabraszewski: front cover, title page, p. 4 (top, left), p. 9, 13; Robert Pernell: p. 4 (top, right), p. 5 (left); Bvasilyev: p. 4 (bottom); Gary Blakeley: p. 4 (bottom); Sonya Etchison: p. 7 (left); Lars Christensen: p. 7 (top, right); Eric Isselée: p. 7 (bottom), 12 (bottom), p. 16 (left); Kucherenko Olena: p. 8; Alle: p. 14 (top); Serg p. 15 (middle, right); Lebedinski Vladislav: p. 15 (bottom); Flavijus: p. 19 (top); Makhnach: p. 19 (bottom), p. 23; Mazzzur: p. 20
Dreamstime: Richard Thomas: p. 4 (bottom); Aidar Ayazbayev: p. 4 (bottom); Ekaterina Kolyzhikhina: p. 7 (top, left); Andres Rodriguez: p. 11; Anna Utekhina: p. 12 (top), p. 16 (right); Piotr Rzeszutek: p. 14; Spencer Berger: p. 14 (bottom);
Istockphoto: p. 5 (right); Greg Nicholas: p. 7 (right); Ana Abejon: p. 11 (middle); Tyson Wirtzfeld: p. 17;
Fotolia: Zbigniew Nowak: p. 6; Julien Vivet: p. 10; Szilagyi Annamaria: p. 15 (middle);
Photolibrary: Marcel Jolibois: p. 15
Q2AMedia Art Bank: 21

Library and Archives Canada Cataloguing in Publication

Piddock, Claire
    Position and direction / Claire Piddock.

(My path to math)
Includes index.
ISBN 978-0-7787-5248-6 (bound).--ISBN 978-0-7787-5295-0 (pbk.)

    1. Topology--Juvenile literature. I. Title. II. Series: My path to math

QA611.13.P53 2009   j514   C2009-905368-3

Library of Congress Cataloging-in-Publication Data

Piddock, Claire.
  Position and direction / Claire Piddock.
    p. cm. -- (My path to math)
  Includes index.
  ISBN 978-0-7787-5248-6 (reinforced lib. bdg. : alk. paper) -- ISBN 978-0-7787-5295-0 (pbk. : alk. paper)
  1. Topology--Juvenile literature. I. Title. II. Series.

  QA611.13.P53 2010
  514--dc22
                                                              2009035496

Crabtree Publishing Company

www.crabtreebooks.com   1-800-387-7650

Printed in China/122009/CT20090903

Published in Canada
Crabtree Publishing
616 Welland Ave.
St. Catharines, ON
L2M 5V6

Published in the United States
Crabtree Publishing
PMB 59051
350 Fifth Avenue, 59th Floor
New York, New York 10118

Published in the United Kingdom
Crabtree Publishing
Maritime House
Basin Road North, Hove
BN41 1WR

Published in Australia
Crabtree Publishing
386 Mt. Alexander Rd.
Ascot Vale (Melbourne)
VIC 3032

Contents

Moving Day

Sam has moved to a new neighborhood with his family. The moving van is **outside** of his new house. Sam is **inside**.

Sam is in his new room. He is putting away his things. He sets a toy fire truck on the **top** shelf. He places his books on the **middle** shelf. He puts his dinosaur toy on the **bottom** shelf.

Sam is inside ▶
this square.

The truck is outside Sam's house.

Activity Box

What else does Sam put on the bottom shelf?

Can you see inside
the moving van?

Up and Down

Sam's room is on the middle floor.
He can go **up** the stairs to the attic.
He can go **down** the stairs to the kitchen.

Sam can see the front yard from
his window. He can see a bird
up in a tree. He can
see a squirrel down
on the ground.

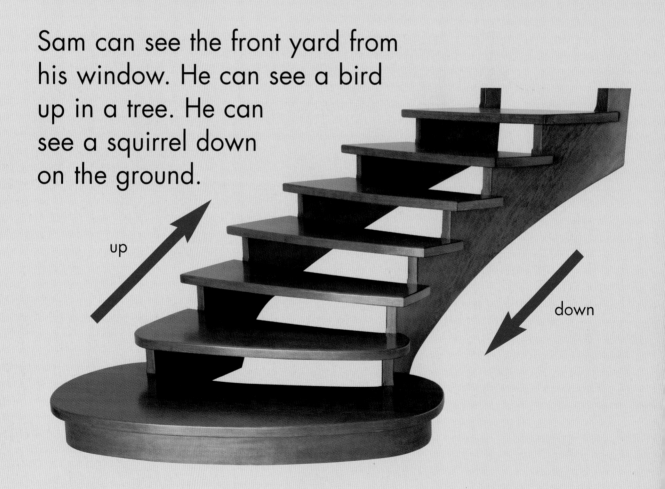

up

down

Activity Box

To climb a tree, do you go up or down first?
To jump into a swimming pool, do you go up or down?

What else might Sam
see when he looks up?

A New Friend

Sam sees a boy out of his window.
The boy on the sidewalk calls up to Sam.
"Come outside!" the boy says.

Sam learns that the boy is his new neighbor.
His name is Jake. They become friends
quickly. Soon they are playing hide-and-seek.
Sam hides first.

Sam stands **behind** a tree, so
the tree hides him. The tree is
in front of Sam. Jake has a
hard time finding him!

Activity Box

Fill in the blanks.

The Sun is _____ the clouds.
The clouds are __ _____ __ the Sun.

Jake looks for Sam in the wrong direction!

Before, After, Between

Now it is Jake's turn. Jake hides **between** some boxes on the porch. But Sam finds him. Here are more things that are between.

I am Jake.

The word "am" is between the word "I" and the word "Jake."

I am 9 years old.

8, 9, 10   The number 9 is between the numbers 8 and 10.
The number 8 is **before** 9.
The number 10 is **after** 9.

22

Activity Box

Sam lives at 22 Red Bird Street.

21, 22, 23   What number is before 23?
What number is after 21?

Jake is peeking from behind the boxes.

Above and Below

Jake invites Sam to play in his back yard. Before going, Sam asks his parents. Sam's mom and dad say yes.

Jake's friend Casey comes out to play, too. They climb up and down the rope ladder. Then they play leap frog.

In the picture, Casey is **above** Jake. Jake is **below** Casey.

above ▶

below ▶

Activity Box

Sam's cat is above Jake's dog. The dog is below the cat. Now, look at the children playing leap frog. What is below them?

In leap frog, players take turns being the bottom "frog."

Over and Under

Jake's mother brings a snack outside. Sam, Jake, and Casey sit at the table. The umbrella is **over** the picnic table. Jake's dog is **under** the table.

The dog waits under the table in case someone drops food.

over ▶

▲
under

Activity Box

In Jake's garden, a bee flies over a flower. A worm is under the flower. Now, look around you. What is over your head? What is under your feet?

The neighbors have a snack between games.

Left and Right

Casey hears her mom calling her home. But Casey says she will come back soon! She lives just across the street. From her house, she can see Jake's house on the **left**. She can see Sam's house on the **right**.

After Casey leaves, the boys drive a remote car. They drive the car left and right in front of their houses. Then they try driving the car up a ramp. The car flies down from the top!

Activity Box

Jake's dog is on the left. Sam's cat is on the right. Look around you. Name something on your left. Name something on your right.

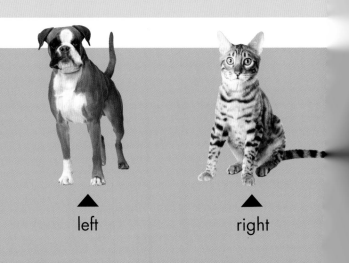

left   right

Name one thing that is found to the left of the sidewalk.

left   right

Directions

Sam's Aunt Bea arrives. She has driven from Canada to help with the move. Sam's new house is in the United States, near Canada. The two countries are **next to** each other!

Aunt Bea shows Sam and Jake her road map. She points out the directions **north**, **south**, **east**, and **west**. She tells them that east is the direction in which the Sun rises. West is the direction in which the Sun sets.

If you face east and turn a quarter turn to the left, you will face north. If you face east and move a quarter turn to the right, you will face south.

East and west are opposites, like hot and cold or big and small. North and south are opposites, too.

Where is your house on the map below? Is it north, east, south, or west of Sam's house?

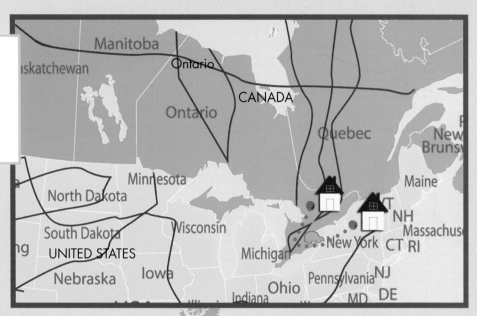

Aunt Bea's home

Sam's new home

A compass rose points out directions on a map.

New Neighborhood

Moving day is fun, from sunrise to sunset. Sam likes his new house. He is glad to see Aunt Bea. Sam, Jake, and Casey are happy to be friends.

Activity Box

Look at the map of Sam's new neighborhood. Use direction words to tell about the places on the map.

Is the school next to the playground?
Is the playground north or south of the school?

Is Jake's house above or below the library?
Is it north or south of the library?

What is to the right of Jake's house?
Is that place east or west of Jake's house?

Describe the location of the school.

Store

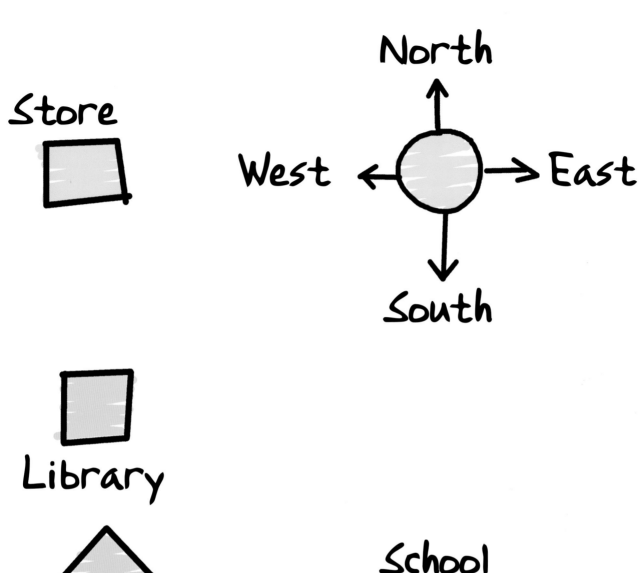

North

West   East

South

Library

Jake's house

School

Playground

Use the glossary and index on the following pages. They will help you understand words that tell us where things are!

Glossary

above In a higher place

after Later in an ordered list of arrangement

before Ahead of; earlier in an ordered list of arrangement

behind In the rear; to the rear

below In a lower place; beneath

between In the space that separates two things

bottom The lowest part or place

down In a lower place

in front of In a leading position; before

inside Within a space

left A direction that is the opposite of right

middle Halfway between two things

next to Nearest or to the side of

outside Not inside or within a given space

over In a higher place

right A direction that is the opposite of left

top The highest point or surface

under In a lower place; beneath

up Toward the sky; toward a higher place

east Where the Sun rises; opposite of west

north To the left as you face the sunrise; opposite of south

south To the right as you face the sunrise; opposite of north

west Where the Sun sets; opposite of east

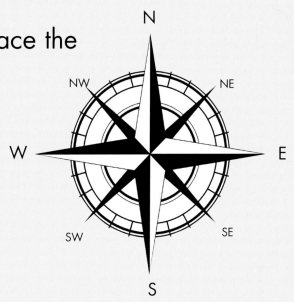

Index